PLAY

and two short pieces

for radio

PLAY

and two short pieces
for radio

*

SAMUEL
BECKETT

FABER & FABER
London

First published in 1964
by Faber and Faber Limited
3 Queen Square London WC1
First published in this edition 1968
Reprinted 1969 and 1971
Printed in Great Britain by
Latimer Trend & Co Ltd Whitstable

ISBN 0 571 08522 9

All applications for performing rights should be addressed to: Curtis Brown Ltd., 13 King Street, London, W.C.2

CONTENTS

PLAY

A Play in One Act

The first performance of *Play* was in German and was given at the Ulmer Theater, Ulm-Donau, Germany on 14th June 1963. The cast was as follows:

w1	First Woman	NANCY ILLIG
w2	Second Woman	SIGRID PFEIFFER
M	Man	GERHARD WINTER

The producer was Deryk Mendel

The first performance of *Play* in England was given by the National Theatre Company on 7th April 1964, with the following cast:

w1	First Woman	ROSEMARY HARRIS
w2	Second Woman	BILLIE WHITELAW
M	Man	ROBERT STEPHENS

The production was by George Devine

Front centre, touching one another, three identical grey urns (see page 24) about one yard high. From each a head protrudes, the neck held fast in the urn's mouth. The heads are those, from left to right as seen from auditorium, of w2, m *and* w1. *They face undeviatingly front throughout the play. Faces so lost to age and aspect as to seem almost part of urns. But no masks.*

Their speech is provoked by a spotlight projected on faces alone. See page 23.

The transfer of light from one face to another is immediate. No blackout, i.e. return to almost complete darkness of opening, except where indicated.

The response to light is immediate.

Faces impassive throughout. Voices toneless except where an expression is indicated.

Rapid tempo throughout.

The curtain rises on a stage in almost complete darkness. Urns just discernible. Five seconds.

Faint spots simultaneously on three faces. Three seconds. Voices faint, largely unintelligible.

w1	Yes, strange, darkness best, and the darker the worse, till all dark, then all well, for the time, but it will come, the time will come, the thing is there, you'll see it, get off me, keep off me, all dark, all still, all over, wiped out——
w2	Yes, perhaps, a shade gone, I suppose, some might say, poor thing, a shade

9

Together.
See page
23

M

gone, just a shade, in the head—(*faint
wild laugh*)—just a shade, but I doubt
it, *I* doubt it, not really, I'm all right,
still all right, do my best, all I can——
Yes, peace, one assumed, all out, all the
pain, all as if . . . never been, it will
come—(*hiccup*)—pardon, no sense in
this, oh I know . . . none the less, one
assumed, peace . . . I mean . . . not
merely all over, but as if . . . never
been——

Spots off. Blackout. Five seconds. Strong spots simultaneously on three faces. Three seconds. Voices normal strength.

w1
w2   *Together.*
M

I said to him, Give her up——
One morning as I was sitting——
We were not long together——

Spots off. Blackout. Five seconds. Spot on w1.

w1: I said to him, Give her up. I swore by all I held most sacred——
Spot from w1 *to* w2.

w2: One morning as I was sitting stitching by the open window she burst in and flew at me. Give him up, she screamed, he's mine. Her photographs were kind to her. Seeing her now for the first time full length in the flesh I understood why he preferred me.
Spot from w2 *to* M.

M: We were not long together when she smelled the rat. Give up that whore, she said, or I'll cut my throat— (*hiccup*) pardon—so help me God. I knew she could have no proof. So I told her I did not know what she was talking about.
Spot from M *to* w2.

w2: What are you talking about? I said, stitching away.

10

Someone yours? Give up whom? I smell you off him, she screamed, he stinks of bitch.

Spot from w2 *to* w1.

w1: Though I had him dogged for months by a first-rate man, no shadow of proof was forthcoming. And there was no denying that he continued as . . . assiduous as ever. This, and his horror of the merely Platonic thing, made me sometimes wonder if I were not accusing him unjustly. Yes.

Spot from w1 *to* M.

M: What have you to complain of? I said. Have I been neglecting you? How could we be together in the way we are if there were someone else? Loving her as I did, with all my heart, I could not but feel sorry for her.

Spot from M *to* w2.

w2: Fearing she was about to offer me violence I rang for Erskine and had her shown out. Her parting words, as he could testify, if he is still living, and has not forgotten, coming and going on the earth, letting people in, showing people out, were to the effect that she would settle my hash. I confess this did alarm me a little, at the time.

Spot from w2 *to* M.

M: She was not convinced. I might have known. I smell her off you, she kept saying. There was no answer to this. So I took her in my arms and swore I could not live without her. I meant it, what is more. Yes, I am sure I did. She did not repulse me.

Spot from M *to* w1.

w1: Judge then of my astoundment when one fine morning, as I was sitting stricken in the morning room, he slunk in, fell on his knees before me, buried his face in my lap and . . . confessed.

11

Spot from w1 *to* M.

M: She put a bloodhound on me, but I had a little chat
with him. He was glad of the extra money.
Spot from M *to* w2.

w2: Why don't you get out, I said, when he started
moaning about his home life, there is obviously
nothing between you any more. Or is there?
Spot from w2 *to* w1.

w1: I confess my first feeling was one of wonderment.
What a male!
Spot from w1 *to* M. *He opens his mouth to speak. Spot
from* M *to* w2.

w2: Anything between us, he said, what do you take me
for, a something machine? And of course with him
no danger of the . . . spiritual thing. Then why don't
you get out? I said. I sometimes wondered if he was
not living with her for her money.
Spot from w2 *to* M.

M: The next thing was the scene between them. I can't
have her crashing in here, she said, threatening to
take my life. I must have looked incredulous. Ask
Erskine, she said, if you don't believe me. But she
threatens to take her own, I said. Not yours? she said.
No, I said, hers. We had fun trying to work this out.
Spot from M *to* w1.

w1: Then I forgave him. To what will love not stoop! I
suggested a little jaunt to celebrate, to the Riviera or
our darling Grand Canary. He was looking pale.
Peaked. But this was not possible just then.
Professional commitments.
Spot from w1 *to* w2.

w2: She came again. Just strolled in. All honey. Licking
her lips. Poor thing. I was doing my nails, by the
open window. He has told me all about it, she said.

12

Who he, I said filing away, and what it? I know
what torture you must be going through, she said,
and I have dropped in to say I bear you no ill-feeling.
I rang for Erskine.
Spot from w2 *to* M.

M: Then I got frightened and made a clean breast of it.
She was looking more and more desperate. She had
a razor in her vanity-bag. Adulterers, take warning,
never admit.
Spot from M *to* w1.

w1: When I was satisfied it was all over I went to have a
gloat. Just a common tart. What he could have
found in her when he had me——
Spot from w1 *to* w2.

w2: When he came again we had it out. I felt like death.
He went on about why he had to tell her. Too risky
and so on. That meant he had gone back to her.
Back to that!
Spot from w2 *to* w1.

w1: Pudding face, puffy, spots, blubber mouth, jowls, no
neck, dugs you could——
Spot from w1 *to* w2.

w2: He went on and on. I could hear a mower. An old
hand mower. I stopped him and said that whatever
I might feel I had no silly threats to offer—but not
much stomach for her leavings either. He thought
that over for a bit.
Spot from w2 *to* w1.

w1: Calves like a flunkey——
Spot from w1 *to* M.

M: When I saw her again she knew. She was looking—
(*hiccup*)—wretched. Pardon. Some fool was cutting
grass. A little rush, then another. The problem was
how to convince her that no . . . revival of

13

intimacy was involved. I couldn't. I might have known. So I took her in my arms and said I could not go on living without her. I don't believe I could have.

Spot from M *to* W2.

w2: The only solution was to go away together. He swore we should as soon as he had put his affairs in order. In the meantime we were to carry on as before. By that he meant as best we could.

Spot from W2 *to* W1.

w1: So he was mine again. All mine. I was happy again. I went about singing. The world——

Spot from W1 *to* M.

M: At home all heart to heart, new leaf and bygones bygones. I ran into your ex-doxy, she said one night, on the pillow, you're well out of that. Rather uncalled for, I thought. I am indeed, sweetheart, I said, I am indeed. God what vermin women. Thanks to you, angel, I said.

Spot from M *to* W1.

w1: Then I began to smell her off him again. Yes.

Spot from W1 *to* W2.

w2: When he stopped coming I was prepared. More or less.

Spot from W2 *to* M.

M: Finally it was all too much. I simply could no longer——

Spot from M *to* W1.

w1: Before I could do anything he disappeared. That meant she had won. That slut! I couldn't credit it. I lay stricken for weeks. Then I drove over to her place. It was all bolted and barred. All grey with frozen dew. On the way back by Ash and Snodland——

14

Spot from W1 *to* M.

M: I simply could no longer——
Spot from M *to* W2.

W2: I made a bundle of his things and burnt them. It was November and the bonfire was going. All night I smelt them smouldering.
Spot off W2. *Blackout. Five seconds. Spots half previous strength simultaneously on three faces. Three seconds. Voices proportionately lower.*

W1 ⎫
W2 ⎬ *Together.* ⎧ Mercy, mercy——
M ⎭ ⎨ To say I am——
⎩ When first this change——
Spots off. Blackout. Five seconds. Spot on M.

M: When first this change I actually thanked God. I thought, It is done, it is said, now all is going out——
Spot from M *to* W1.

W1: Mercy, mercy, tongue still hanging out for mercy. It will come. You haven't seen me. But you will. Then it will come.
Spot from W1 *to* W2.

W2: To say I am not disappointed, no, I am. I had anticipated something better. More restful.
Spot from W2 *to* W1.

W1: Or you will weary of me. Get off me.
Spot from W1 *to* M.

M: Down, all going down, into the dark, peace is coming, I thought, after all, at last, I was right, after all, thank God, when first this change.
Spot from M *to* W2.

W2: Less confused. Less confusing. At the same time I prefer this to . . . the other thing. Definitely. There are endurable moments.
Spot from W2 *to* M.

M: I thought.
Spot from M *to* W2.

w2: When you go out—and I go out. Some day you will tire of me and go out . . . for good.
Spot from W2 *to* W1.

w1: Hellish half-light.
Spot from W1 *to* M.

M: Peace, yes, I suppose, a kind of peace, and all that pain as if . . . never been.
Spot from M *to* W2.

w2: Give me up, as a bad job. Go away and start poking and pecking at someone else. On the other hand——
Spot from W2 *to* W1.

w1: Get off me! (*Vehement.*) Get off me!
Spot from W1 *to* M.

M: It will come. Must come. There is no future in this.
Spot from M *to* W2.

w2: On the other hand things may disimprove, there is that danger.
Spot from W2 *to* M.

M: Oh of course I know now——
Spot from M *to* W1.

w1: Is it that I do not tell the truth, is that it, that some day somehow I may tell the truth at last and then no more light at last, for the truth?
Spot from W1 *to* W2.

w2: You might get angry and blaze me clean out of my wits. Mightn't you?
Spot from W2 *to* M.

M: I know now, all that was just . . . play. And all this? When will all this——
Spot from M *to* W1.

w1: Is that it?
Spot from W1 *to* W2.

w2: Mightn't you?
Spot from w2 *to* M.

M: All this, when will all this have been . . . just play?
Spot from M *to* w1.

w1: I can do nothing . . . for anybody . . . any more . . .
thank God. So it must be something I have to say.
How the mind works still!
Spot from w1 *to* w2.

w2: But I doubt it. It would not be like you somehow.
And you must know I am doing my best. Or don't
you?
Spot from w2 *to* M.

M: Perhaps they have become friends. Perhaps
sorrow——
Spot from M *to* w1.

w1: But I have said all I can. All you let me. All I——
Spot from w1 *to* M.

M: Perhaps sorrow has brought them together.
Spot from M *to* w2.

w2: No doubt I make the same mistake as when it was
the sun that shone, of looking for sense where
possibly there is none.
Spot from w2 *to* M.

M: Perhaps they meet, and sit, over a cup of that green
tea they both so loved, without milk or sugar, not
even a squeeze of lemon——
Spot from M *to* w2.

w2: Are you listening to me? Is anyone listening to me?
Is anyone looking at me? Is anyone bothering about
me at all?
Spot from w2 *to* M.

M: Not even a squeeze of——
Spot from M *to* w1.

w1: Is it something I should do with my face, other than

utter? Weep?

Spot from w1 *to* w2.

w2: Am I taboo, I wonder. Not necessarily, now that all danger is averted. That poor creature—I can hear her—that poor creature——

Spot from w2 *to* w1.

w1: Bite off my tongue and swallow it? Spit it out? Would that placate you? How the mind works still to be sure!

Spot from w1 *to* M.

M: Meet, and sit, now in the one dear old place, now in the other, and sorrow together, and compare— (*hiccup*) pardon—happy memories.

Spot from M *to* w1.

w1: If only I could think. There is no sense in this . . . either, none whatsoever. I can't.

Spot from w1 *to* w2.

w2: That poor creature who tried to seduce you, what ever became of her, do you suppose?—I can hear her. Poor thing.

Spot from w2 *to* M.

M: Personally I always preferred Lipton's.

Spot from M *to* w1.

w1: And that all is falling, all fallen, from the beginning, on empty air. Nothing being asked at all. No one asking me for anything at all.

Spot from w1 *to* w2.

w2: They might even feel sorry for me, if they could see me. But never so sorry as I for them.

Spot from w2 *to* w1.

w1: I can't.

Spot from w1 *to* w2.

w2: Kissing their sour kisses.

Spot from w2 *to* M.

18

M: I pity them in any case, yes, compare my lot with
theirs, however blessed, and——
Spot from M *to* W1.

W1: I can't. The mind won't have it. It would have to
go. Yes.
Spot from W1 *to* M.

M: Pity them.
Spot from M *to* W2.

W2: What do you do when you go out? Sift?
Spot from W2 *to* M.

M: Am I hiding something? Have I lost——
Spot from M *to* W1.

W1: She had means, I fancy, though she lived like a pig.
Spot from W1 *to* W2.

W2: Like dragging a great roller, on a scorching day.
The strain . . . to get it moving, momentum
coming——
Spot off W2. *Blackout. Three seconds. Spot on* W2.

W2: Kill it and strain again.
Spot from W2 *to* M.

M: Have I lost . . . the thing you want? Why go out?
Why go——
Spot from M *to* W2.

W2: And you perhaps pitying me, thinking, Poor thing,
she needs a rest.
Spot from W2 *to* W1.

W1: Perhaps she has taken him away to live . . .
somewhere in the sun.
Spot from W1 *to* M.

M: Why go down? Why not——
Spot from M *to* W2.

W2: I don't know.
Spot from W2 *to* W1.

W1: Perhaps she is sitting somewhere, by the open

19

window, her hands folded in her lap, gazing down
out over the olives——
Spot from w1 *to* M.

M: Why not keep on glaring at me without ceasing? I
might start to rave and—(*hiccup*)—bring it up for
you. Par——
Spot from M *to* w2.

w2: No.
Spot from w2 *to* M.

M: —don.
Spot from M *to* w1.

w1: Gazing down out over the olives, then the sea,
wondering what can be keeping him, growing cold.
Shadow stealing over everything. Creeping. Yes.
Spot from w1 *to* M.

M: To think we were never together.
Spot from M *to* w2.

w2: Am I not perhaps a little unhinged already?
Spot from w2 *to* w1.

w1: Poor creature. Poor creatures.
Spot from w1 *to* M.

M: Never woke together, on a May morning, the first to
wake to wake the other two. Then in a little
dinghy——
Spo from M *to* w1.

w1: Penitence, yes, at a pinch, atonement, one was
resigned, but no, that does not seem to be the point
either.
Spot from w1 *to* w2.

w2: I say, Am I not perhaps a little unhinged already?
(*Hopefully*.) Just a little? (*Pause*.) I doubt it.
Spot from w2 *to* M.

M: A little dinghy——
Spot from M *to* w1.

w1: Silence and darkness were all I craved. Well, I get a certain amount of both. They being one. Perhaps it is more wickedness to pray for more.
Spot from w1 *to* m.

m: A little dinghy, on the river, I resting on my oars, they lolling on air-pillows in the stern . . . sheets. Drifting. Such fantasies.
Spot from m *to* w1.

w1: Hellish half-light.
Spot from w1 *to* w2.

w2: A shade gone. In the head. Just a shade. I doubt it.
Spot from w2 *to* m.

m: We were not civilized.
Spot from m *to* w1.

w1: Dying for dark—and the darker the worse. Strange.
Spot from w1 *to* m.

m: Such fantasies. Then. And now——
Spot from m *to* w2.

w2: *I* doubt it.
Pause. Peal of wild low laughter from w2 *cut short as spot from her to* w1.

w1: Yes, and the whole thing there, all there, staring you in the face. You'll see it. Get off me. Or weary.
Spot from w1 *to* m.

m: And now, that you are . . . mere eye. Just looking. At my face. On and off.
Spot from m *to* w1.

w1: Weary of playing with me. Get off me. Yes.
Spot from w1 *to* m.

m: Looking for something. In my face. Some truth. In my eyes. Not even.
Spot from m *to* w2. *Laugh as before from* w2 *cut short as spot from her to* m.

m: Mere eye. No mind. Opening and shutting on me.

21

Am I as much——

Spot off M. *Blackout. Three seconds. Spot on* M.

M: Am I as much as . . . being seen?

Spot off M. *Blackout. Five seconds. Faint spots simultaneously on three faces. Three seconds. Voices faint, largely unintelligible.*

w1 ⎫
w2 ⎬ *Together.* ⎧ Yes, strange, etc.
M ⎭ ⎨ Yes, perhaps, etc.
 ⎩ Yes, peace, etc.

Repeat play.

M: (*closing repeat*). Am I as much as . . . being seen?

Spot off M. *Blackout. Five seconds. Strong spots simultaneously on three faces. Three seconds. Voices normal strength.*

w1 ⎫
w2 ⎬ *Together.* ⎧ I said to him, Give her up——
M ⎭ ⎨ One morning as I was sitting——
 ⎩ We were not long together——

Spots off Blackout. Five seconds. Spot on M.

M: We were not long together——

Spot off M. *Blackout. Five seconds.*

CURTAIN

22

LIGHT

The source of light is single and must not be situated outside the ideal space (stage) occupied by its victims.

The optimum position for the spot is at the centre of the footlights, the faces being thus lit at close quarters and from below.

When exceptionally three spots are required to light the three faces simultaneously, they should be as a single spot branching into three.

Apart from these moments a single mobile spot should be used, swivelling at maximum speed from one face to another as required.

The method consisting in assigning to each face a separate fixed spot is unsatisfactory in that it is less expressive of a unique inquisitor than the single mobile spot.

CHORUS

w1	Yes strange	darkness best	and the darker	the worse
w2	Yes perhaps	a shade gone	I suppose	some might say
M	Yes peace	one assumed	all out	all the pain

w1	till all dark	then all well	for the time	but it will come
w2	poor thing	a shade gone	just a shade	in the head
M	all as if	never been	it will come	(*hiccup*) pardon

w1	the time will come	the thing is there	you'll see it
w2	(*laugh – – – – –*)	just a shade	but I doubt it
M	no sense in this	oh I know	none the less

w1	get off me	keep off me	all dark	all still
w2	*I* doubt it	not really	I'm all right	still all right
M	one assumed	peace I mean	not merely	all over

w1	all over	wiped out——
w2	do my best	all I can——
M	but as if	never been——

23

URNS

In order for the urns to be only one yard high, it is necessary either that traps be used, enabling the actors to stand below stage level, or that they kneel throughout play, the urns being open at the back.

Should traps be not available, and the kneeling posture found impracticable, the actors should stand, the urns be enlarged to full length and moved back from front to mid-stage, the tallest actor setting the height, the broadest the breadth, to which the three urns should conform.

The sitting posture results in urns of unacceptable bulk and is not to be considered.

REPEAT

The repeat may be an exact replica of first statement or it may present an element of variation.

In other words, the light may operate the second time exactly as it did the first (exact replica) or it may try a different method (variation).

The London production (and in a lesser degree the Paris production) opted for the variation with following deviations from first statement:

1. Introduction of an abridged chorus, cut short on laugh of w2, to open fragment of second repeat.

2. Light less strong in repeat and voices correspondingly lower, giving the following schema, where A is the highest level of light and voice and E the lowest:

c	First chorus.	
A	First part of 1.	} 1
B	Second part of 1.	
D	Second chorus.	
B	First part of Repeat 1.	} Repeat 1
C	Second part of Repeat 1.	
E	Abridged chorus.	} Fragment of Repeat 2
C	Fragment of Repeat 2	

3. Breathless quality in voices from beginning of Repeat 1 and increasing to end of play.

4. Changed order of speeches in repeat as far as this is compatible with unchanged continuity for actors. E.g. the order of interrogation w1, w2, M, w2, w1, M at opening of 1 becomes w2, w1, M, w2, M, w1 at opening of repeat, and so on if and as desired.

WORDS AND MUSIC

Words and Music was first broadcast on the
B.B.C. on 13th November 1962. The cast was as
follows:
Croak   FELIX FELTON
Words   PATRICK MAGEE
The producer was MICHAEL BAKEWELL

MUSIC: *Small orchestra softly tuning up.*
WORDS: Please! (*Tuning. Louder.*) Please! (*Tuning dies away.*) How much longer cooped up here in the dark? (*With loathing.*) With you! (*Pause.*) Theme. . . . (*Pause.*) Theme . . . sloth. (*Pause. Rattled off, low.*) Sloth is of all the passions the most powerful passion and indeed no passion is more powerful than the passion of sloth, this is the mode in which the mind is most affected and indeed—(*Burst of tuning. Loud, imploring.*) Please! (*Tuning dies away. As before.*) The mode in which the mind is most affected and indeed in no mode is the mind more affected than in this, by passion we are to understand a movement of the soul pursuing or fleeing real or imagined pleasure or pain pleasure or pain real or imagined pleasure or pain, of all these movements and who can number them of all these movements and they are legion sloth is the most urgent and indeed by no movement is the soul more urged than by this by this by this to and from by no movement the soul more urged than by this to and—— (*Pause.*) From. (*Pause.*) Listen! (*Distant sound of rapidly shuffling carpet slippers.*) At last! (*Shuffling louder. Burst of tuning.*) Hsst!
Tuning dies away. Shuffling louder. Silence.
CROAK: Joe.
WORDS: (*humble*). My Lord.
CROAK: Bob.

MUSIC: *Humble muted adsum.*

CROAK: My comforts! Be friends! (*Pause.*) Bob.

MUSIC: *As before.*

CROAK: Joe.

WORDS: (*as before*). My Lord.

CROAK: Be friends! (*Pause.*) I am late, forgive. (*Pause.*) The face. (*Pause.*) On the stairs. (*Pause.*) Forgive. (*Pause.*) Joe.

WORDS: (*as before*). My Lord.

CROAK: Bob.

MUSIC: *As before.*

CROAK: Forgive. (*Pause.*) In the tower. (*Pause.*) The face. (*Long pause.*) Theme tonight. . . . (*Pause.*) Theme tonight . . . love. (*Pause.*) Love. (*Pause.*) My club. (*Pause.*) Joe.

WORDS: (*as before*). My Lord.

CROAK: Love. (*Pause. Thump of club on ground.*) Love!

WORDS: (*orotund*). Love is of all the passions the most powerful passion and indeed no passion is more powerful than the passion of love. (*Clears throat.*) This is the mode in which the mind is most strongly affected and indeed in no mode is the mind more strongly affected than in this. (*Pause.*)

CROAK: *Rending sigh. Thump of club.*

WORDS: (*as before*). By passion we are to understand a movement of the mind pursuing or fleeing real or imagined pleasure or pain. (*Clears throat.*) Of all——

CROAK: (*anguished*). Oh!

WORDS: (*as before*). Of all these movements then and who can number them and they are legion sloth is the LOVE is the most urgent and indeed by no manner of movement is the soul more urged

28

than by this, to and——
Violent thump of club.

CROAK: Bob.

WORDS: From.
Violent thump of club.

CROAK: Bob!

MUSIC: *As before.*

CROAK: Love!

MUSIC: *Rap of baton on stand. Soft music worthy of foregoing, great expression, with audible groans and protestations—"No!" "Please!" etc.—from* WORDS. *Pause.*

CROAK: (*anguished*). Oh! (*Thump of club.*) Louder!

MUSIC: *Loud rap of baton and as before fortissimo, all expression gone, drowning* WORDS' *protestations. Pause.*

CROAK: My comforts! (*Pause.*) Joe sweet.

WORDS: (*as before*). Arise then and go now the manifest unanswerable——

CROAK: *Groans.*

WORDS: —to wit this love what is this love that more than all the cursed deadly or any other of its great movers so moves the soul and soul what is this soul that more than by any of its great movers is by love so moved? (*Clears throat. Prosaic.*) Love of woman, I mean, if that is what my Lord means.

CROAK: Alas!

WORDS: What? (*Pause. Very rhetorical.*) Is love the word? (*Pause. Do.*) Is soul the word? (*Pause. Do.*) Do we mean love, when we say love? (*Pause. Pause. Do.*) Soul, when we say soul?

CROAK: (*anguished*). Oh! (*Pause.*) Bob dear.

WORDS: Do we? (*With sudden gravity.*) Or don't we?

29

CROAK: (*imploring*). Bob!

MUSIC: *Rap of baton. Love and soul music, with just audible protestations—"No!" "Please!" "Peace!" etc.—from* WORDS. *Pause.*

CROAK: (*anguished*). Oh! (*Pause.*) My balms! (*Pause.*) Joe.

WORDS: (*humble*). My Lord.

CROAK: Bob.

MUSIC: *Adsum as before.*

CROAK: My balms! (*Pause.*) Age. (*Pause.*) Joe. (*Pause. Thump of club.*) Joe.

WORDS: (*as before*). My Lord.

CROAK: Age!

Pause.

WORDS: (*faltering*). Age is . . . age is when . . . old age I mean . . . if that is what my Lord means . . . is when . . . if you're a man . . . were a man . . . huddled . . . nodding . . . the ingle . . . waiting——

Violent thump of club.

CROAK: Bob. (*Pause.*) Age. (*Pause. Violent thump of club.*) Age!

MUSIC: *Rap of baton. Age music, soon interrupted by violent thump.*

CROAK: Together. (*Pause. Thump.*) Together! (*Pause. Violent thump.*) Together, dogs!

MUSIC: *Long la.*

WORDS: (*imploring*). No!

Violent thump.

CROAK: Dogs!

MUSIC: *La.*

WORDS: (*trying to sing*). As is when . . . to a man . . .

MUSIC: *Improvement of above.*

WORDS: (*trying to sing this*). Age is when to a man . . .

30

MUSIC: *Suggestion for following.*

WORDS: (*trying to sing this*). Huddled o'er . . . the ingle. . . . (*Pause. Violent thump. Trying to sing.*) Waiting for the hag to put the . . . pan . . . in the bed. . . .

MUSIC: *Improvement of above.*

WORDS: (*trying to sing this*). Waiting for the hag to put the pan in the bed. . . .

MUSIC: *Suggestion for following.*

WORDS: (*trying to sing this*). And bring the . . . arrowroot. . . . (*Pause. Violent thump. As before.*) And bring the toddy. . . .
Pause. Tremendous thump.

CROAK: Dogs!

MUSIC: *Suggestion for following.*

WORDS: (*trying to sing this*). She comes in the ashes. . . . (*Imploring.*) No!

MUSIC: *Repeats suggestion.*

WORDS: (*trying to sing this*). She comes in the ashes who loved could not be . . . won or. . . .
Pause.

MUSIC: *Repeats end of previous suggestion.*

WORDS: (*trying to sing this*). Or won not loved . . . (*wearily*) . . . or some other trouble. . . . (*Pause. Trying to sing.*) Comes in the ashes like in that old——

MUSIC: *Interrupts with improvement of this and brief suggestion.*

WORDS: (*trying to sing this*). Comes in the ashes like in that old light . . . her face . . . in the ashes. . . .
Pause.

CROAK: *Groans.*

MUSIC: *Suggestion for following.*

WORDS: (*trying to sing this*). That old moonlight . . . on

31

the earth . . . again.
Pause.

MUSIC: *Further brief suggestion.*
Silence.

CROAK: *Groans.*

MUSIC: *Plays air through alone, then invites* WORDS *with opening, pause, invites again and finally accompanies very softly.*

WORDS: (*trying to sing, softly*).

> Age is when to a man
> Huddled o'er the ingle
> Shivering for the hag
> To put the pan in the bed
> And bring the toddy
> She comes in the ashes
> Who loved could not be won
> Or won not loved
> Or some other trouble
> Comes in the ashes
> Like in that old light
> The face in the ashes
> That old starlight
> On the earth again.

Long pause.

CROAK: (*murmur*). The face. (*Pause.*) The face. (*Pause.*) The face. (*Pause.*) The face.

MUSIC: *Rap of baton and warmly sentimental, about one minute.*
Pause.

CROAK: The face.

WORDS: (*cold*). Seen from above in that radiance so cold and faint. . . .
Pause.

MUSIC: *Warm suggestion from above for above.*

32

WORDS: (*disregarding, cold*). Seen from above at such close quarters in that radiance so cold and faint with eyes so dimmed by . . . what had passed, its quite . . . piercing beauty is a little. . . .
Pause.

MUSIC: *Renews timidly previous suggestion.*

WORDS: (*interrupting, violently*). Peace!

CROAK: My comforts! Be friends!
Pause.

WORDS: . . . blunted. Some moments later however, such are the powers of recuperation at this age, the head is drawn back to a distance of two or three feet, the eyes widen to a stare and begin to feast again. (*Pause.*) What then is seen would have been better seen in the light of day, that is incontestable. But how often it has, in recent months, how often, at all hours, under all angles, in cloud and shine, been seen I mean. And there is, is there not, in that clarity of silver . . . that clarity of silver . . . is there not . . . my Lord. . . . (*Pause.*) Now and then the rye, swayed by a light wind, casts and withdraws its shadow.
Pause.

CROAK: *Groans.*

WORDS: Leaving aside the features of lineaments proper, matchless severally and in their ordonnance——

CROAK: *Groans.*

WORDS: —flare of the black disordered hair as though spread wide on water, the brows knitted in a groove suggesting pain but simply concentration more likely all things considered on some consummate inner process, the eyes of course closed in keeping with this, the lashes . . .

C 33

CROAK: *(pause)* . . . the nose . . . *(pause)* . . . nothing, a little pinched perhaps, the lips. . . .

CROAK: *(anguished).* Lily!

WORDS: . . . tight, a gleam of tooth biting on the under, no coral, no swell, whereas normally. . . .

CROAK: *Groans.*

WORDS: . . . the whole so blanched and still that were it not for the great white rise and fall of the breasts, spreading as they mount and then subsiding to their natural . . . aperture——

MUSIC: *Irrepressible burst of spreading and subsiding music with vain protestations—"Peace!" "No!" "Please!" etc.—from* WORDS. *Triumph and conclusion.*

WORDS: *(gently expostulatory).* My Lord! *(Pause. Faint thump of club.)* I resume, so wan and still and so ravished away that it seems no more of the earth than Mira in the Whale, at her tenth and greatest magnitude on this particular night and shining coldly down—as we say, looking up. *(Pause.)* Some moments later however, such are the powers——

CROAK: *(anguished).* No!

WORDS: —the brows uncloud, the lips part and the eyes . . . *(pause)* . . . the brows uncloud, the nostrils dilate, the lips part and the eyes . . . *(pause)* . . . a little colour comes back into the cheeks and the eyes . . . *(reverently)* . . . open. *(Pause.)* Then down a little way. . . . *(Pause. Change to poetic tone. Low.)*

> Then down a little way
> Through the trash
> To where . . . towards where. . . .

Pause.

34

MUSIC: *Discreet suggestion for above.*
WORDS: (*trying to sing this*).

> Then down a little way
> Through the trash
> Towards where. . . .

Pause.

MUSIC: *Discreet suggestion for following.*
WORDS: (*trying to sing this*).

> All dark no begging
> No giving no words
> No sense no need. . . .

Pause.

MUSIC: *More confident suggestion for following.*
WORDS: (*trying to sing this*).

> Through the scum
> Down a little way
> To where one glimpse
> Of that wellhead.

Pause.

MUSIC: *Invites with opening, pause, invites again and finally accompanies very softly.*
WORDS: (*trying to sing, softly*).

> Then down a little way
> Through the trash
> Towards where
> All dark no begging
> No giving no words
> No sense no need
> Through the scum
> Down a little way
> To whence one glimpse
> Of that wellhead.

(*Pause. Shocked.*) My Lord! (*Sound of club let fall. As before.*) My Lord! (*Shuffling slippers,*

35

with halts. *They die away. Long pause*.) Bob.
(*Pause*.) Bob!

MUSIC: *Brief rude retort.*

WORDS: Music. (*Imploring*.) Music!
Pause.

MUSIC: *Rap of baton and statement with elements already used or wellhead alone.*
Pause.

WORDS: Again. (*Pause. Imploring*.) Again!

MUSIC: *As before or only very slightly varied.*
Pause.

WORDS: *Deep sigh.*

CURTAIN

36

CASCANDO

A Radio Piece for Music and Voice

Cascando was first broadcast in French on R.T.F. The Speakers were:

Opener	ROGER BLIN
Voice	JEAN MARTIN

The General direction was by ROGER BLIN

OPENER : (*cold*). It is the month of May . . . for me.
(*Pause.*)
Correct.
(*Pause.*)
I open.

VOICE : (*low, panting*). —story . . . if you could finish it
. . . you could rest . . . sleep . . . not before . . .
oh I know . . . the ones I've finished . . .
thousands and one . . . all I ever did . . . in my
life . . . with my life . . . saying to myself . . .
finish this one . . . it's the right one . . . then rest
. . . sleep . . . no more stories . . . no more
words . . . and finished it . . . and not the right
one . . . couldn't rest . . . straight away another
. . . to begin . . . to finish . . . saying to myself
finish this one . . . then rest . . . this time . . .
it's the right one . . . this time . . . you have it
. . . and finished it . . . and not the right one . . .
couldn't rest . . . straight away another . . . but
this one . . . it's different . . . I'll finish it . . .
I've got it . . . Woburn . . . I resume . . . a long
life . . . already . . . say what you like . . . a few
misfortunes . . . that's enough . . . five years
later . . . ten . . . I don't know . . . Woburn . . .
he's changed . . . not enough . . . recognizable . . .
in the shed . . . yet another . . . waiting for
night . . . night to fall . . . to go out . . . go on . . .
elsewhere . . . sleep elsewhere . . . it's slow . . .
he lifts his head . . . now and then . . . his eyes
. . . to the window . . . it's darkening . . . earth

39

darkening . . . it's night . . . he gets up . . .
knees first . . . then up . . . on his feet . . . slips
out . . . Woburn . . . same old coat . . . right the
sea . . . left the hills . . . he has the choice . . .
he has only——

OPENER: (*with* VOICE). And I close.

(*Silence.*)

I open the door.

MUSIC: –

OPENER: (*with* MUSIC). And I close.

(*Silence.*)

I open both.

VOICE: (*together*). —on . . . getting on . . . finish . . . don't

MUSIC: –

give up . . . then rest . . . sleep . . . not before . . .

– –

finish . . . this time . . . it's the right one . . . you

– –

have it . . . you've got it . . . it's there . . .

– –

somewhere . . . you've got him . . . follow him

– –

him . . . don't lose him . . . Woburn story . . .

– –

getting on . . . finish . . . then sleep . . . no more

– –

stories . . . no more words . . . come on . . . next

– –

thing . . . he——

– – – – – – – – – – – – –

OPENER: (*with* VOICE *and* MUSIC). And I close.

Silence.

I start again.

VOICE: —down . . . gentle slope . . . boreen . . . giant

aspens . . . wind in the boughs . . . faint sea . . .
Woburn . . . same old coat . . . he goes on . . .
stops . . . not a soul . . . not yet . . . night too
bright . . . say what you like . . . he goes on . . .
hugging the bank . . . same old stick . . . he goes
down . . . falls . . . on purpose or not . . . can't
see . . . he's down . . . that's what counts . . .
face in the mud . . . arms spread . . . that's the
idea . . . already . . . there already . . . no not
yet . . . he gets up . . . knees first . . . hands flat
. . . in the mud . . . head sunk . . . then up . . .
on his feet . . . huge bulk . . . come on . . . he
goes on . . . he goes down . . . come on . . . in
his head . . . what's in his head . . . a hole . . . a
shelter . . . a hollow . . . in the dunes . . . a
cave . . . vague memory . . . in his head . . . a of
cave . . . he goes down . . . no more trees . . .
no more bank . . . he's changed . . . not enough
. . . night too bright . . . soon the dunes . . . no
more cover . . . not a soul . . . not——
Silence.

MUSIC: –
Silence.

VOICE: (*together.*)——rest . . . sleep . . . no more stories
MUSIC: –

. . . no more words . . . don't give up . . . this

– –

time . . . it's the right one . . . we're there . . .

– –

I'm there . . . somewhere . . . Woburn . . . I've

– –

got him . . . don't lose him . . . follow him . . . to

– –

the end . . . come on . . . this time . . . it's the

- -

right one . . . finish . . . sleep . . . Woburn . . .

- -

come on——

- - - - -

Silence.

OPENER: So, at will.

They say, It's in his head.

No. I open.

VOICE: —falls . . . again . . . on purpose or not . . .
can't see . . . he's down . . . that's what matters
. . . face in the sand . . . arms spread . . . bare
dunes . . . not a scrub . . . same old coat . . .
night too bright . . . say what you like . . . sea
louder . . . thunder . . . manes of foam . . .
Woburn . . . his head . . . what's in his head . . .
peace . . . peace again . . . in his head . . . no
further . . . no more searching . . . sleep . . . no
not yet . . . he gets up . . . knees first . . . hands
flat . . . in the sand . . . head sunk . . . then up
. . . on his feet . . . huge bulk . . . same old
broadbrim . . . jammed down . . . come on . . .
he goes on . . . ton weight . . . in the sand . . .
knee-deep . . . he goes down . . . sea——

OPENER: (*with* VOICE). And I close.

Silence.

I open the other.

MUSIC: -

OPENER: (*with* MUSIC). And I close.

Silence.

So, at will.

It's my life, I live on that.

Pause.

Correct.

42

Pause.

What do I open?

They say, He opens nothing, he has nothing to open, it's in his head.

They don't see me, they don't see what I do, they don't see what I have, and they say, He opens nothing, he has nothing to open, it's in his head.

I don't protest any more, I don't say any more, There is nothing in my head.

I don't answer any more.

I open and close.

VOICE: —lights . . . of the land . . . the island . . . the sky . . . he need only . . . lift his head . . . his eyes . . . he'd see them . . . shine on him . . . but no . . . he——

Silence.

MUSIC: (*brief*).– – – – – – – – – – – – – – – – –

Silence.

OPENER: They say, That is not his life, he does not live on that. They don't see me, they don't see what my life is, they don't see what I live on, and they say, That is not his life, he does not live on that.

Pause.

I have lived on it . . . till I'm old.

Old enough.

Listen.

VOICE: (*weakening*).—this time . . . I'm there . . . Woburn . . . it's him . . . I've seen him . . . I've got him . . . come on . . . same old coat . . . he goes down . . . falls . . . falls again . . . on purpose or not . . . can't see . . . he's down . . . that's what counts. . . . come on——

43

OPENER: (*with* VOICE). Full strength.

VOICE: —face . . . in the stones . . . no more sand . . .
all stones . . . that's the idea . . . we're there . . .
this time . . . no not yet . . . he gets up . . .
knees first . . . hands flat . . . in the stones . . .
head sunk . . . then up . . . on his feet . . . huge
bulk . . . Woburn . . . faster . . . he goes on . . .
he goes down . . . he——
Silence.

MUSIC: (*weakening*). – – – – – – – – – – – – – – –

OPENER: (*with* MUSIC). Full strength.

MUSIC: –
Silence.

OPENER: That's not all.
I open both.
Listen.

VOICE: (*together*). —sleep . . . no further . . . no more
MUSIC: – – – – – – – – – – – – – – – – – –

searching . . . to find him . . . in the dark . . . to
– –

see him . . . to say him . . . for whom . . . that's
– –

it . . . no matter . . . never him . . . never right . . .
– –

start again . . . in the dark . . . done with that
– –

. . . this time . . . it's the right one . . . we're
– –

there . . . nearly . . . finish——
– – – – – – – – – – – – – –

Silence.

OPENER: From one world to another, it's as though they
drew together. We have not much further to go.
Good.

44

VOICE: (together). —nearly . . . I've got him . . . I've
MUSIC: — — — — — — — — — — — — — — — — —

see him . . . I've said him . . . we're there . . .
— — — — — — — — — — — — — — — — — — — —

nearly . . . no more stories . . . all false . . . this
— — — — — — — — — — — — — — — — — — — —

time . . . it's the right one . . . I have it . . . finish
— — — — — — — — — — — — — — — — — — — —

. . . sleep . . . Woburn . . . it's him . . . I've got
him . . .
— — — — — — — — — — — — — — — — — — — —

follow him . . . to——
— — — — — — — — —

Silence.

OPENER: Good.

Pause.

Yes, correct, the month of May.
You know, the reawakening.

Pause.

I open.

VOICE: —no tiller . . . no thwarts . . . no oars . . .
afloat . . . sucked out . . . then back . . .
aground . . . drags free . . . out . . . Woburn . . .
he fills it . . . flat out . . . face in the bilge . . .
arms spread . . . same old coat . . . hands
clutching . . . the gunnels . . . no . . . I don't
know . . . I see him . . . he clings on . . . out to
sea . . . heading nowhere . . . for the island . . .
then no more . . . else——

Silence.

MUSIC: — — — — — — — — — — — — — — — — — —

Silence

OPENER: They said, It's his own, it's his voice, it's in his
head.

45

Pause.

VOICE: —faster . . . out . . . driving out . . . rearing . . .
plunging . . . heading nowhere . . . for the
island . . . then no more . . . elsewhere . . .
anywhere . . . heading anywhere . . . lights——
Silence.

OPENER: No resemblance.

I answered, And that . . .

MUSIC: (*brief*) –
Silence.

OPENER: . . . is that mine too?

But I don't answer any more.

And they don't say anything any more.

They have quit.

Good.

Pause.

Yes, correct, the month of May, the close of
May.

The long days.

Pause.

I open.

Pause.

I'm afraid to open.

But I must open.

So I open.

VOICE: —come on . . . Woburn . . . arms spread . . .
same old coat . . . face in the bilge . . . he clings
on . . . island gone . . . far astern . . . heading
out . . . open sea . . . land gone . . . his head
. . . what's in his head . . . Woburn——

OPENER: (*with* VOICE). Come on! Come on!

VOICE: —at last . . . we're there . . no further . . . no
more searching . . . in the dark . . . elsewhere
. . . always elsewhere . . . we're there . . . nearly

46

       . . . Woburn . . . hang on . . . don't let go . . .
       lights gone . . . of the land . . . all gone . . .
       nearly all . . . too far . . . too late . . . of the sky
       . . . those . . . if you like . . . he need only . . .
       turn over . . . he'd see them . . . shine on him
       . . . but no . . . he clings on . . . Woburn . . .
       he's changed . . . nearly enough——
       Silence.

MUSIC: –

OPENER: (*with* MUSIC). God.

MUSIC: –

       Silence.

OPENER: God God.
       Pause.
       There was a time I asked myself, what is it.
       There were times I answered, It's the outing.
       Two outings.
       Then the return.
       Where?
       To the village.
       To the inn.
       Two outings, then at last the return, to the
       village, to the inn, by the only road that leads
       there.
       An image, like any other.
       But I don't answer any more.
       I open.

VOICE: (*together*). —don't let go . . . finish . . . it's the
MUSIC: – – – – – – – – – – – – – – – – – – –

       right one . . . this time . . . I have it . . . we're

– –

       there . . . Woburn . . . nearly——

– – – – – – – – – – – – – –

OPENER: (*with* VOICE *and* MUSIC). As though they had

47

linked their arms.

VOICE: *(together).* —sleep . . . no more stories . . . come
MUSIC:

on . . . Woburn . . . it's him . . . see him . . . say

him . . . to the end . . . don't let go——

OPENER: *(with* VOICE *and* MUSIC*).* Good.

VOICE: *(together).* —nearly . . . just a few more . . . a
MUSIC:

more . . . I'm there . . . nearly . . . Woburn . . .

it's him . . . it was him . . . I've got him . . .

nearly——

OPENER: *(with* VOICE *and* MUSIC, *fervently).* Good!

VOICE: *(together).* —this time . . . it's the right one . . .
MUSIC:

finish . . . no more stories . . . sleep . . . we're

there . . . nearly . . . just a few more . . . don't let

go . . . Woburn . . . he clings on . . . come on . . .

come on——

Silence.

CURTAIN